MAR 0 1 2019

Y0-CCJ-266

GRAPHIC LIBRARY™

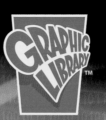

GRAPHIC SCIENCE

THE ILLUMINATING WORLD OF LIGHT

WITH MAX AXIOM™ SUPER SCIENTIST

4D An Augmented Reading Science Experience

by Emily Sohn | illustrated by Nick Derington

Consultant:
Leslie Flynn, PhD
Science Education, Chemistry
University of Minnesota

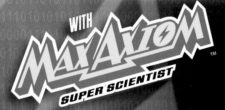

Graphic Library is published by Capstone Press,
1710 Roe Crest Drive, North Mankato, Minnesota 56003.
www.mycapstone.com

Library of Congress Cataloging-in-Publication Data is available on the Library of Congress website.

ISBN: 978-1-5435-5868-5 (library binding)
ISBN: 978-1-5435-6001-5 (paperback)
ISBN: 978-1-5435-5878-4 (eBook PDF)

Summary: In graphic novel format, follows the adventures of Max Axiom
as he explains the science behind light.

Art Director and
Designer
Bob Lentz

Cover Artist
Tod Smith

Editor
Christopher Harbo

Photo Credits
Capstone Studio: Karon Dubke, 29, back cover;
iStockphoto: dra_schwartz, 23; Shutterstock: Jo-Hanna Wienert, 13

1 Ask an adult to download the app.

 Capstone 4D
Education

2 Scan any page with the star.

3 Enjoy your cool stuff!

— OR —

Use this password at capstone4D.com

light.58685

TABLE OF CONTENTS

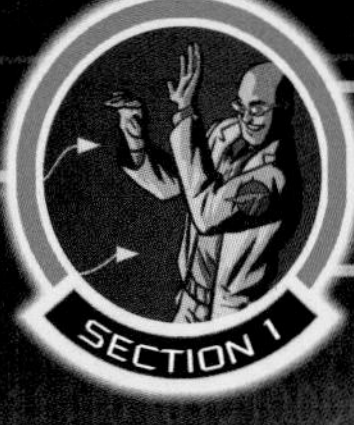
SECTION 1

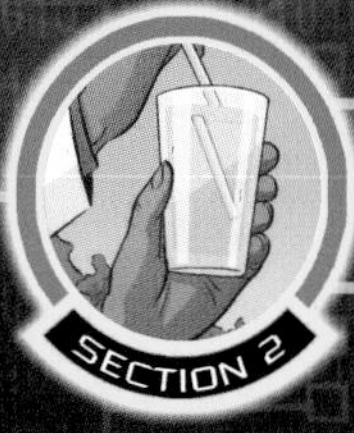
SECTION 2

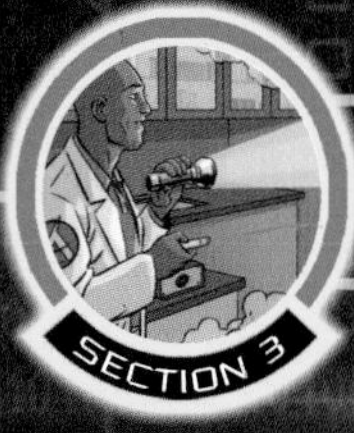
SECTION 3

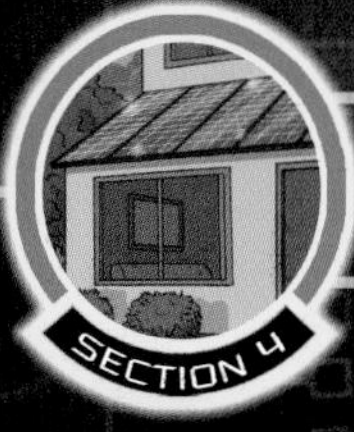
SECTION 4

SECTION 1 I SEE THE LIGHT

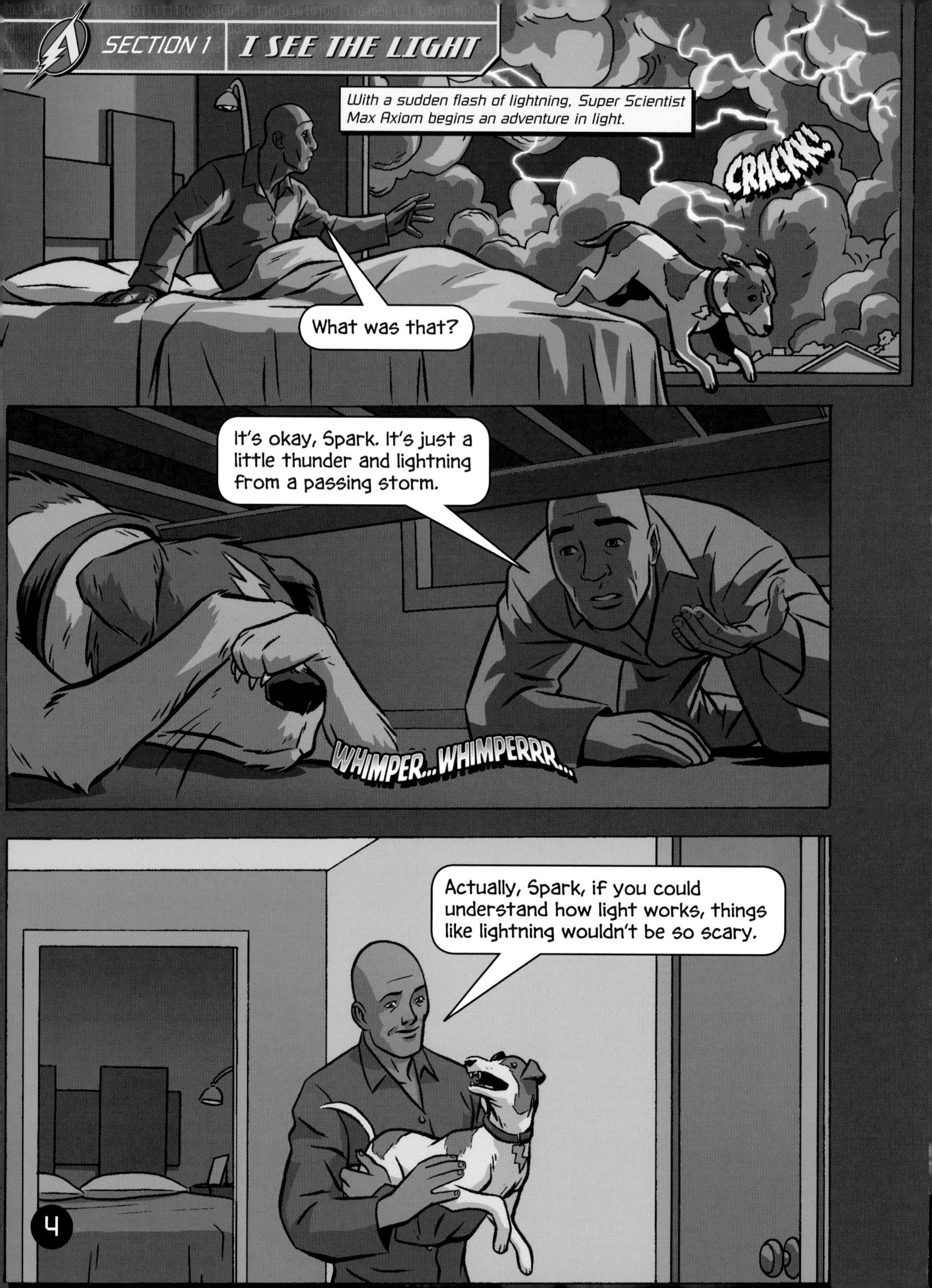

With a sudden flash of lightning, Super Scientist Max Axiom begins an adventure in light.
CRACK!
What was that?
It's okay, Spark. It's just a little thunder and lightning from a passing storm.
WHIMPER...WHIMPERRR...
Actually, Spark, if you could understand how light works, things like lightning wouldn't be so scary.

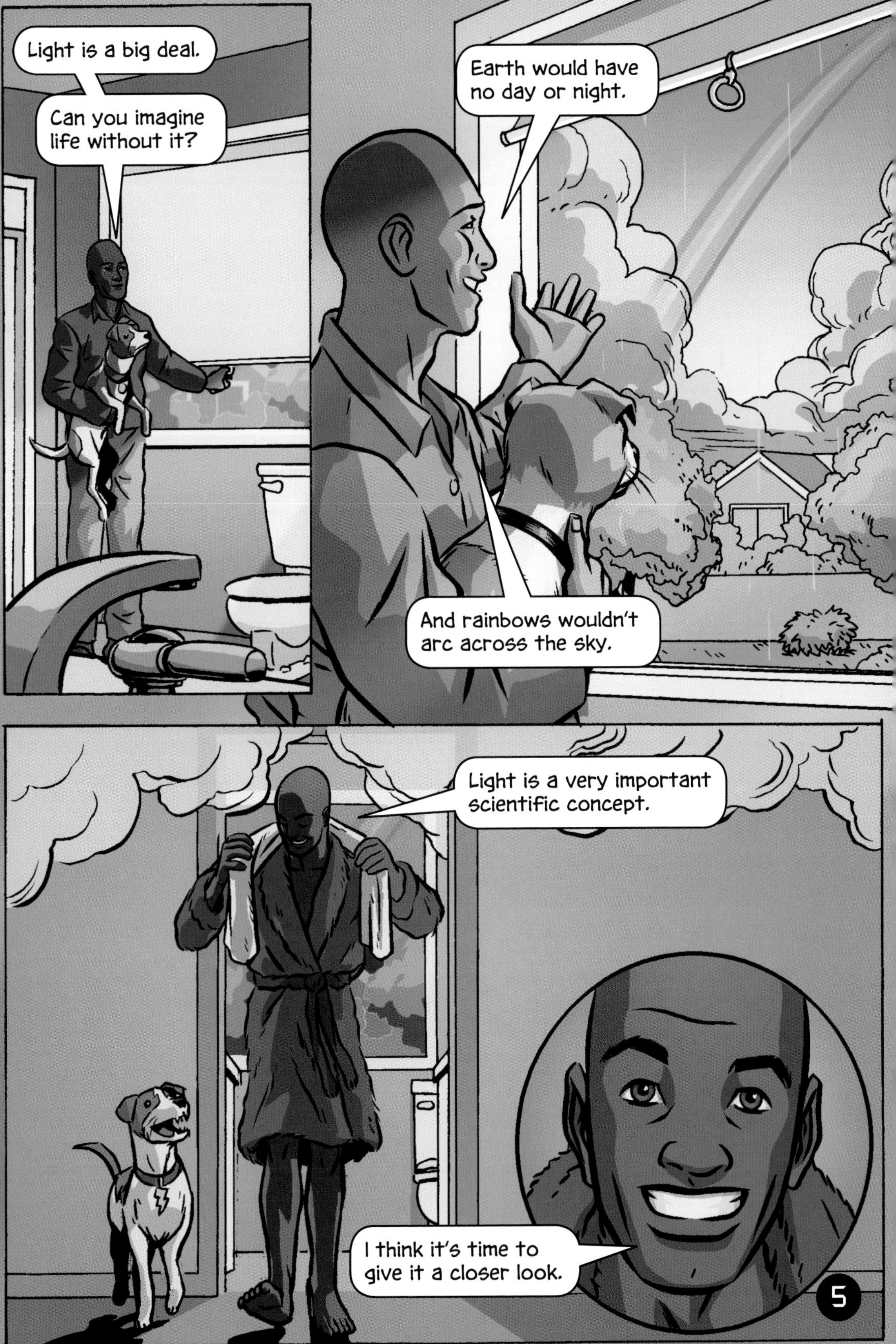
Light is a big deal.
Can you imagine life without it?
Earth would have no day or night.
And rainbows wouldn't arc across the sky.
Light is a very important scientific concept.
I think it's time to give it a closer look.

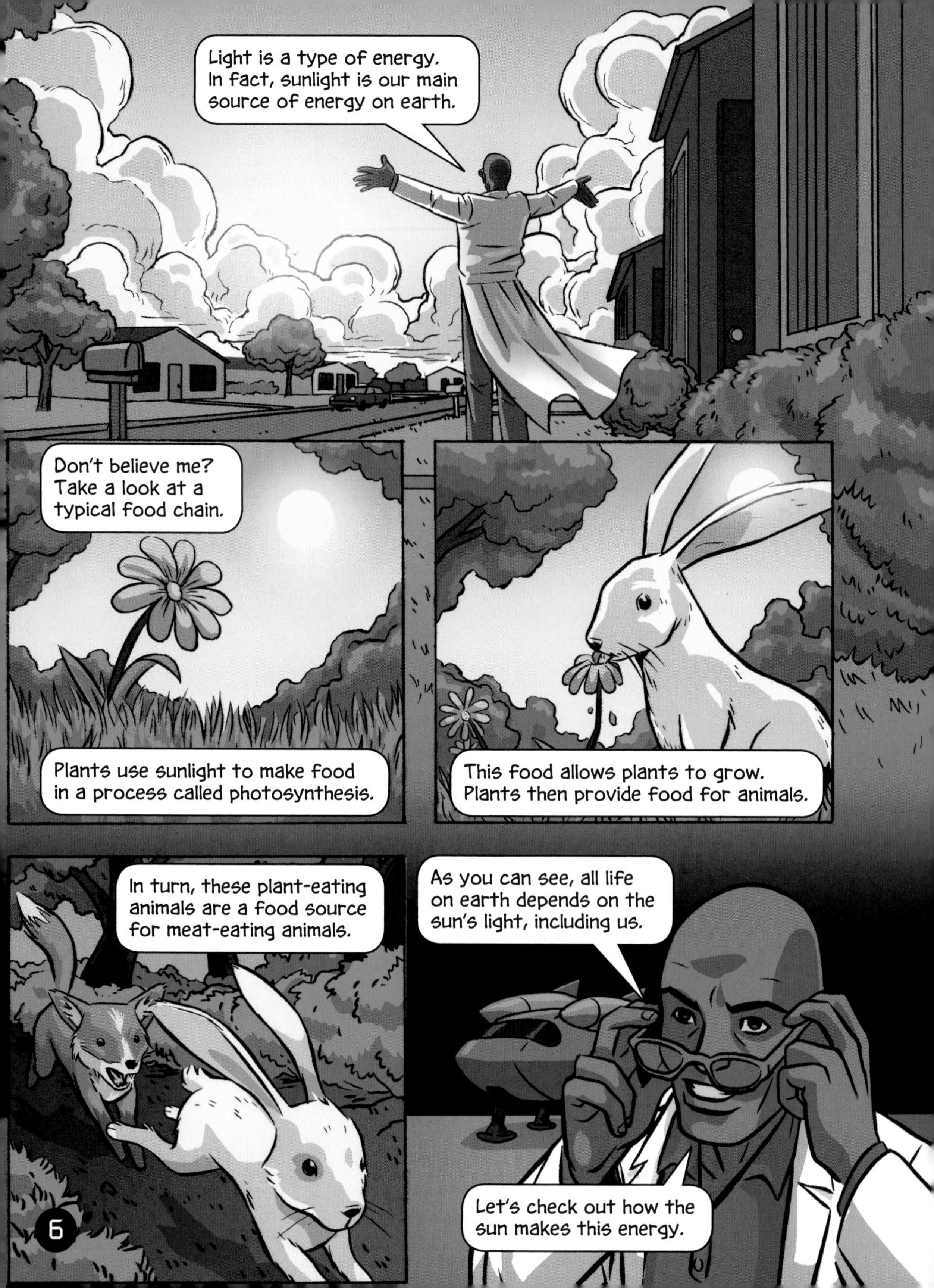
Light is a type of energy. In fact, sunlight is our main source of energy on earth.
Don't believe me? Take a look at a typical food chain.
Plants use sunlight to make food in a process called photosynthesis.
This food allows plants to grow. Plants then provide food for animals.
In turn, these plant-eating animals are a food source for meat-eating animals.
As you can see, all life on earth depends on the sun's light, including us.
Let's check out how the sun makes this energy.

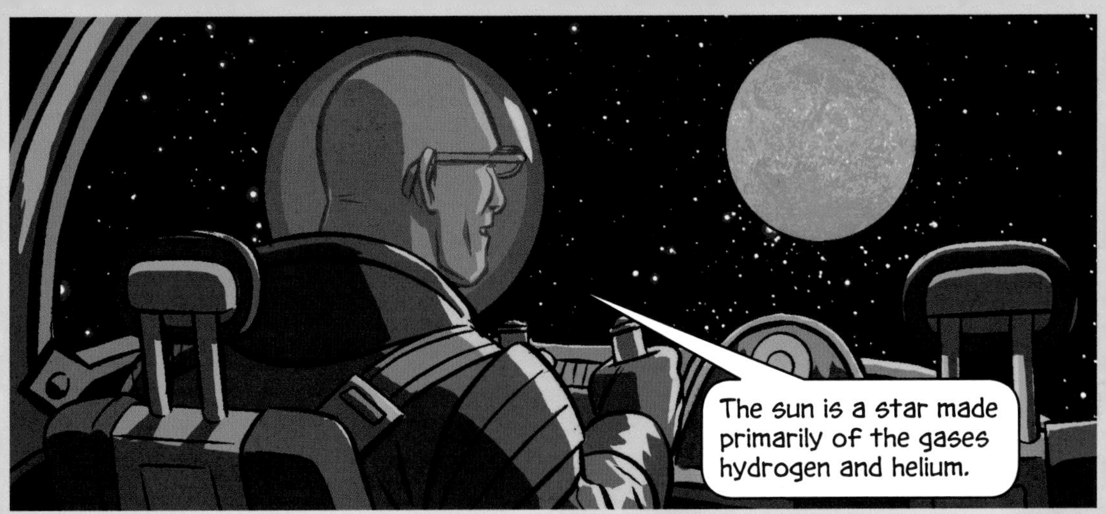
The sun is a star made primarily of the gases hydrogen and helium.

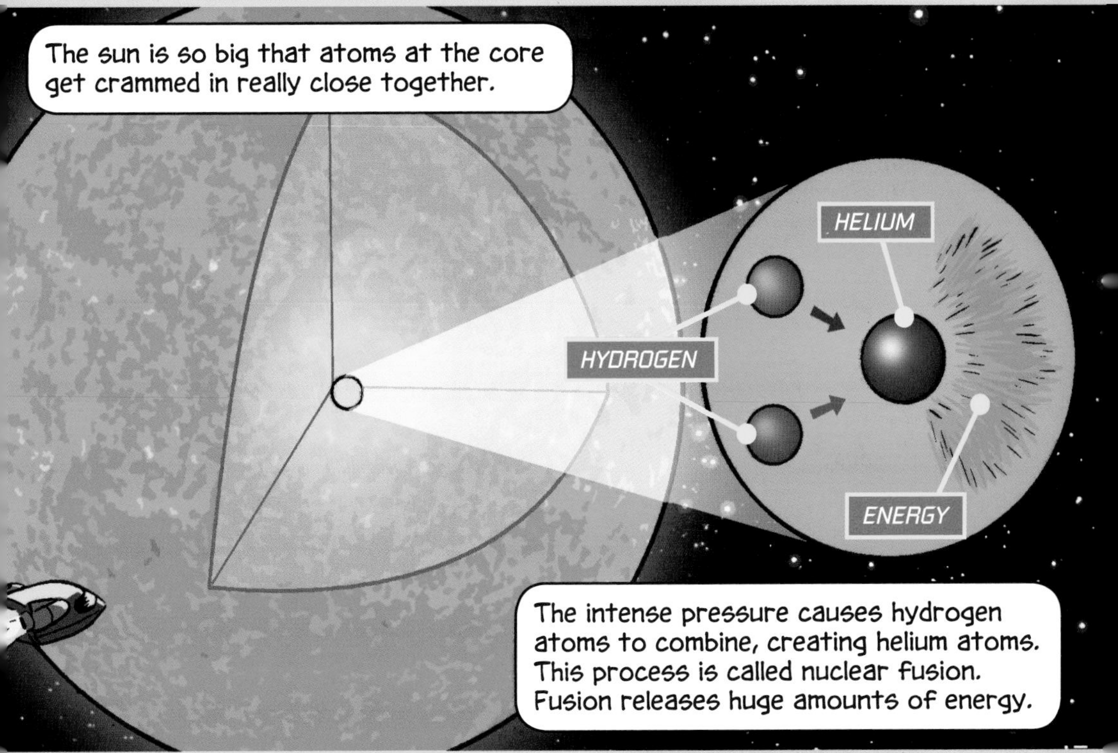
The sun is so big that atoms at the core get crammed in really close together.
HELIUM
HYDROGEN
ENERGY
The intense pressure causes hydrogen atoms to combine, creating helium atoms. This process is called nuclear fusion. Fusion releases huge amounts of energy.

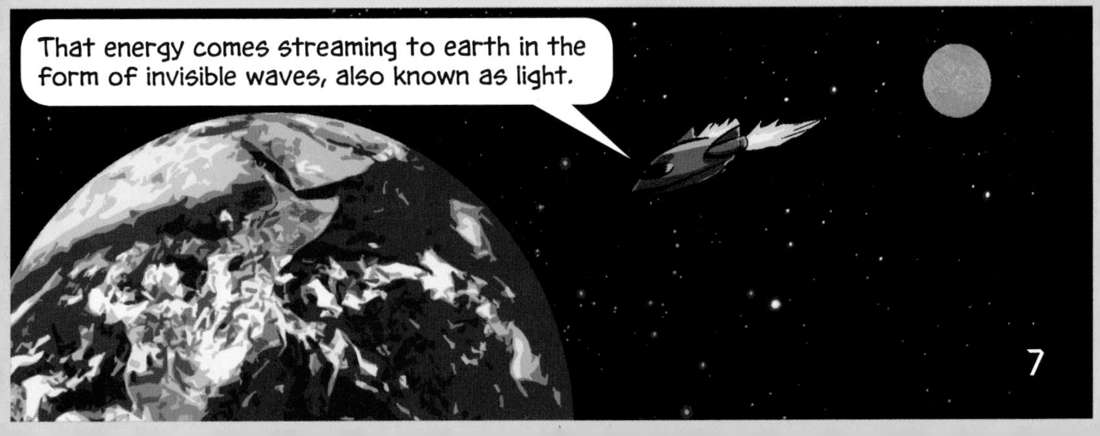
That energy comes streaming to earth in the form of invisible waves, also known as light.

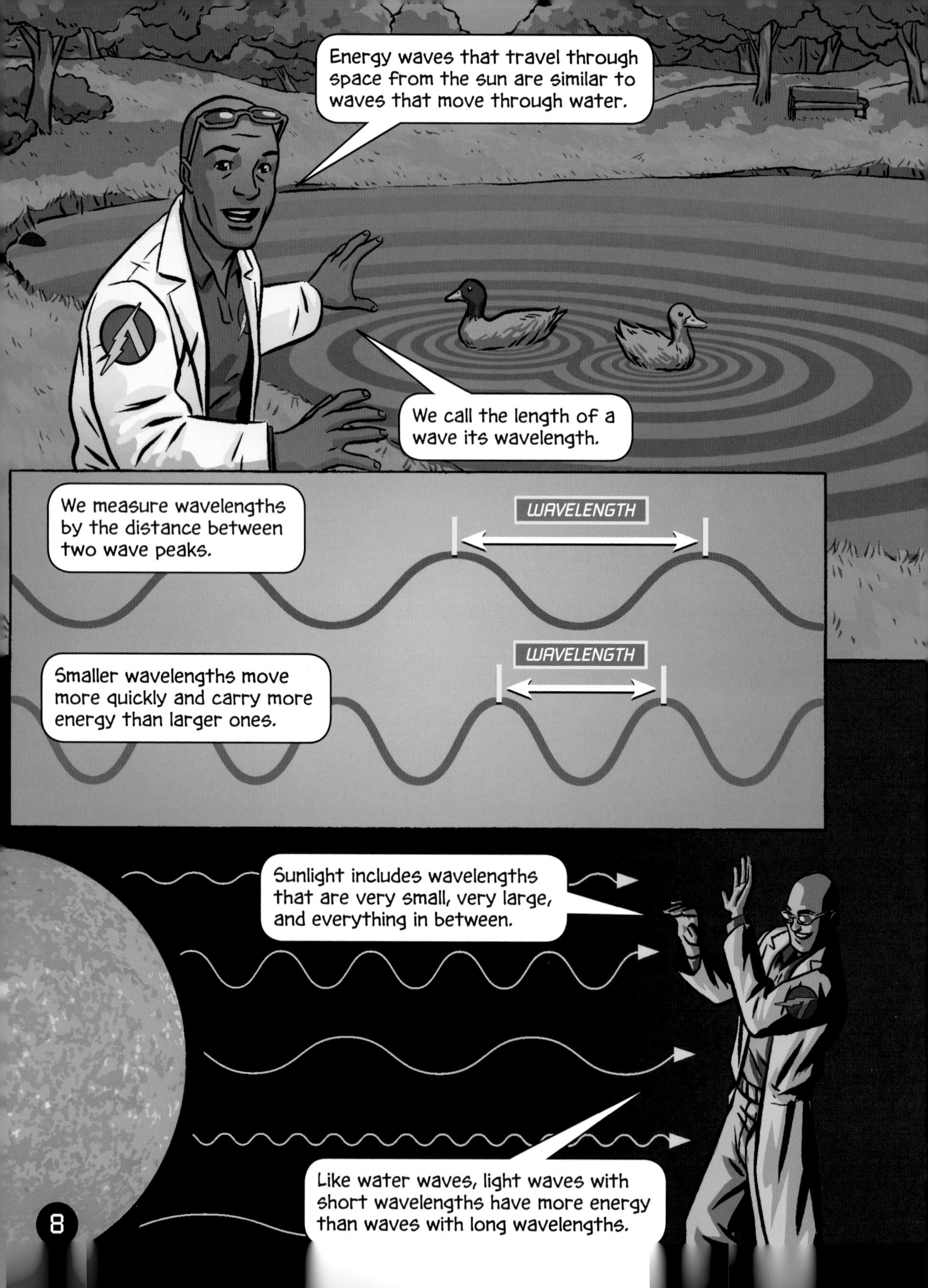
Energy waves that travel through space from the sun are similar to waves that move through water.
We call the length of a wave its wavelength.
We measure wavelengths by the distance between two wave peaks.
WAVELENGTH
Smaller wavelengths move more quickly and carry more energy than larger ones.
WAVELENGTH
Sunlight includes wavelengths that are very small, very large, and everything in between.
Like water waves, light waves with short wavelengths have more energy than waves with long wavelengths.

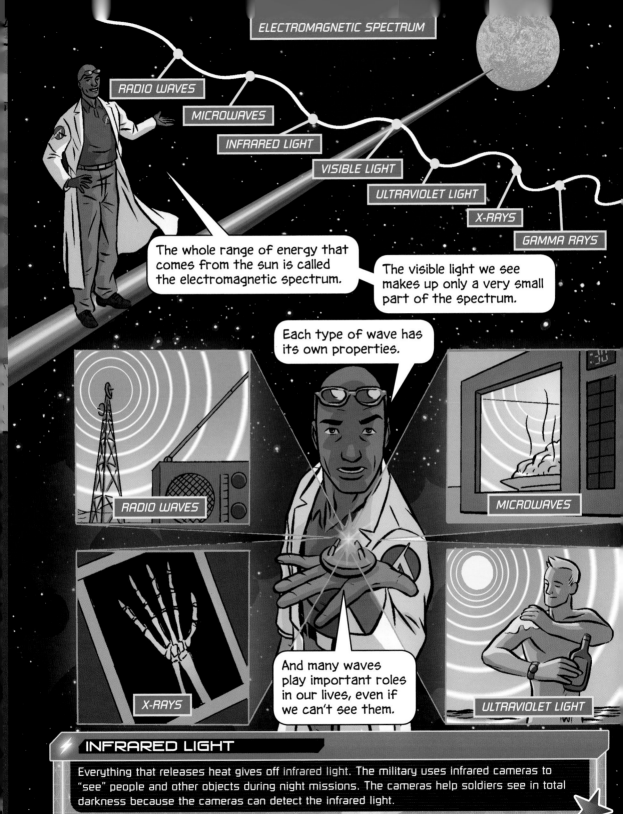

ELECTROMAGNETIC SPECTRUM

RADIO WAVES

MICROWAVES

INFRARED LIGHT

VISIBLE LIGHT

ULTRAVIOLET LIGHT

X-RAYS

GAMMA RAYS

The whole range of energy that comes from the sun is called the electromagnetic spectrum.

The visible light we see makes up only a very small part of the spectrum.

Each type of wave has its own properties.

RADIO WAVES

MICROWAVES

X-RAYS

And many waves play important roles in our lives, even if we can't see them.

ULTRAVIOLET LIGHT

INFRARED LIGHT

Everything that releases heat gives off infrared light. The military uses infrared cameras to "see" people and other objects during night missions. The cameras help soldiers see in total darkness because the cameras can detect the infrared light.

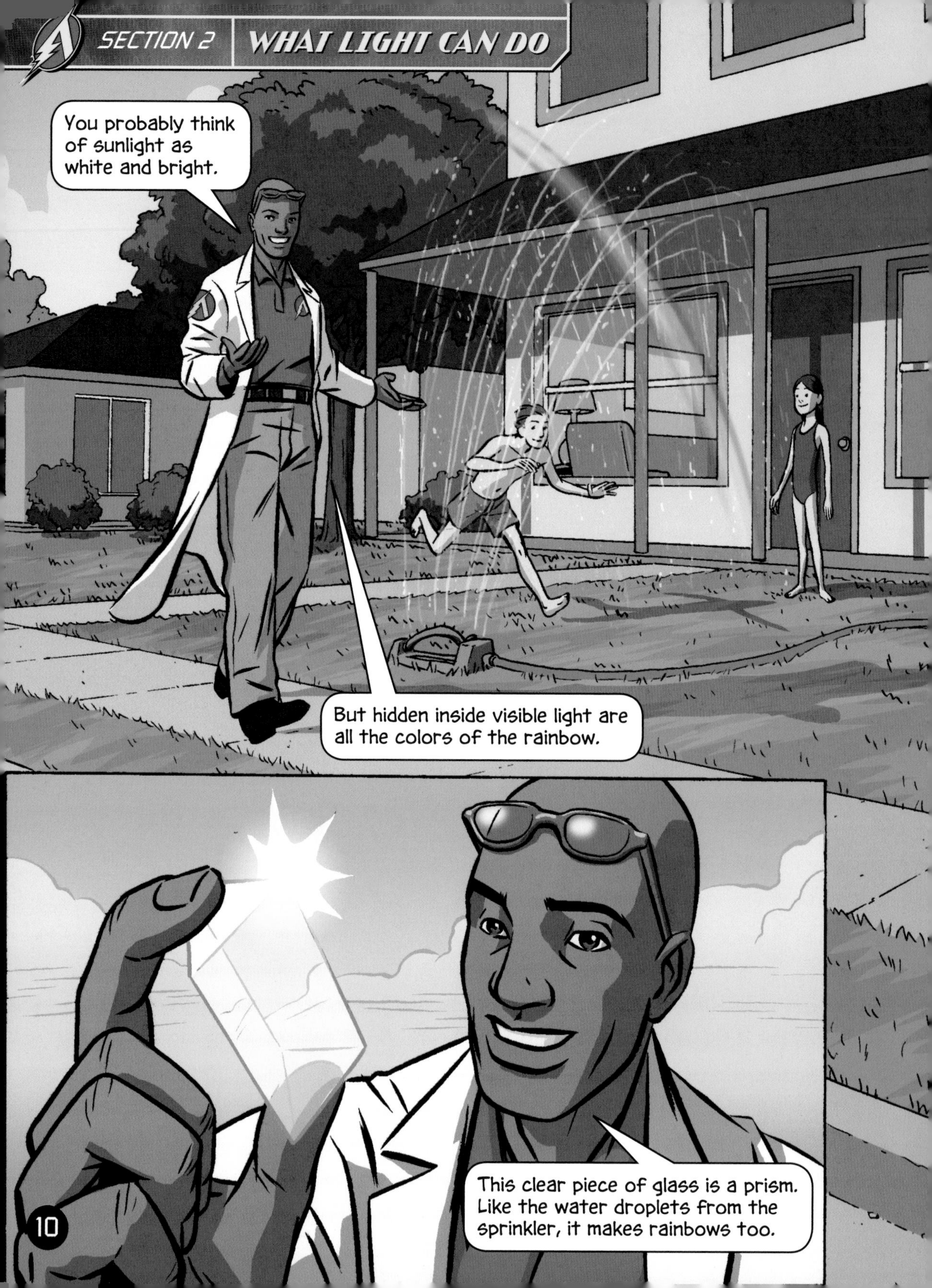
You probably think of sunlight as white and bright.
But hidden inside visible light are all the colors of the rainbow.
This clear piece of glass is a prism. Like the water droplets from the sprinkler, it makes rainbows too.

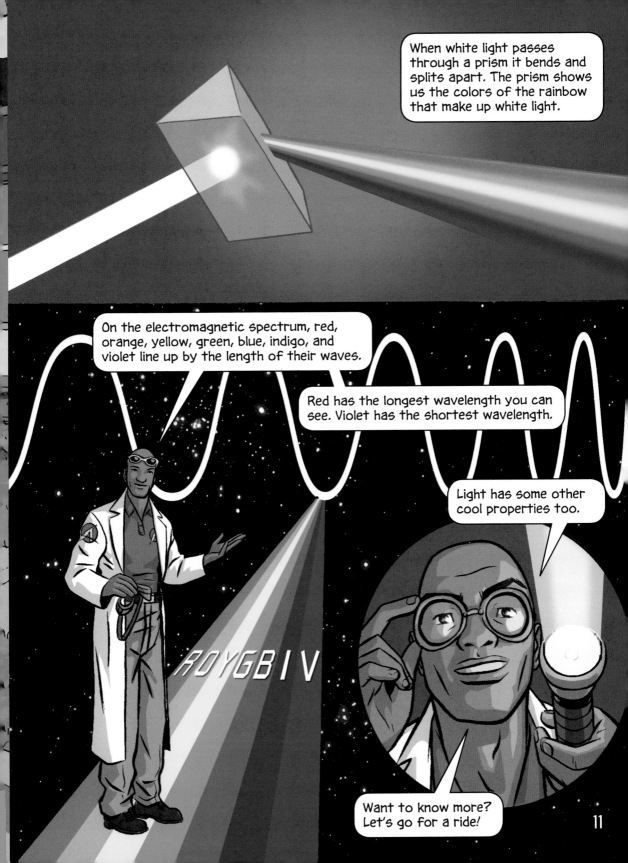

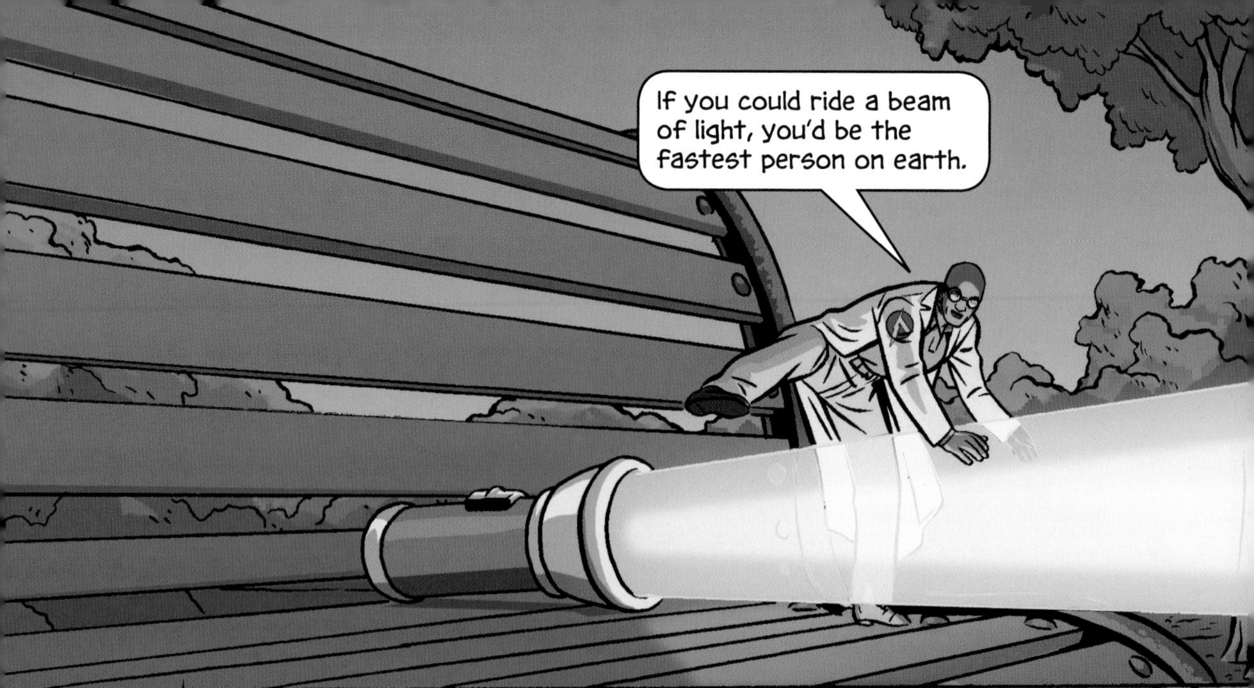
If you could ride a beam of light, you'd be the fastest person on earth.

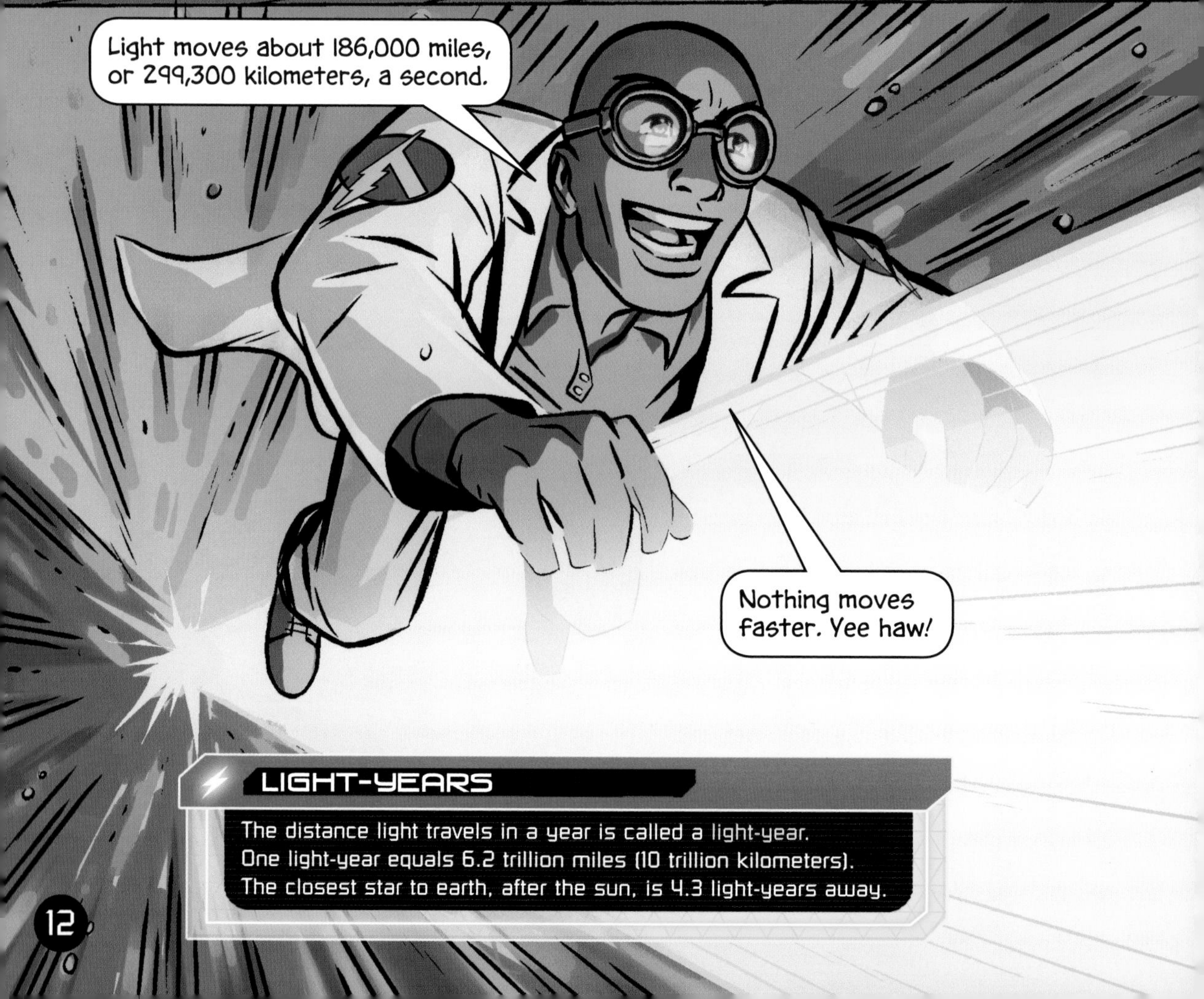
Light moves about 186,000 miles, or 299,300 kilometers, a second.
Nothing moves faster. Yee haw!

LIGHT-YEARS

The distance light travels in a year is called a light-year. One light-year equals 6.2 trillion miles (10 trillion kilometers). The closest star to earth, after the sun, is 4.3 light-years away.

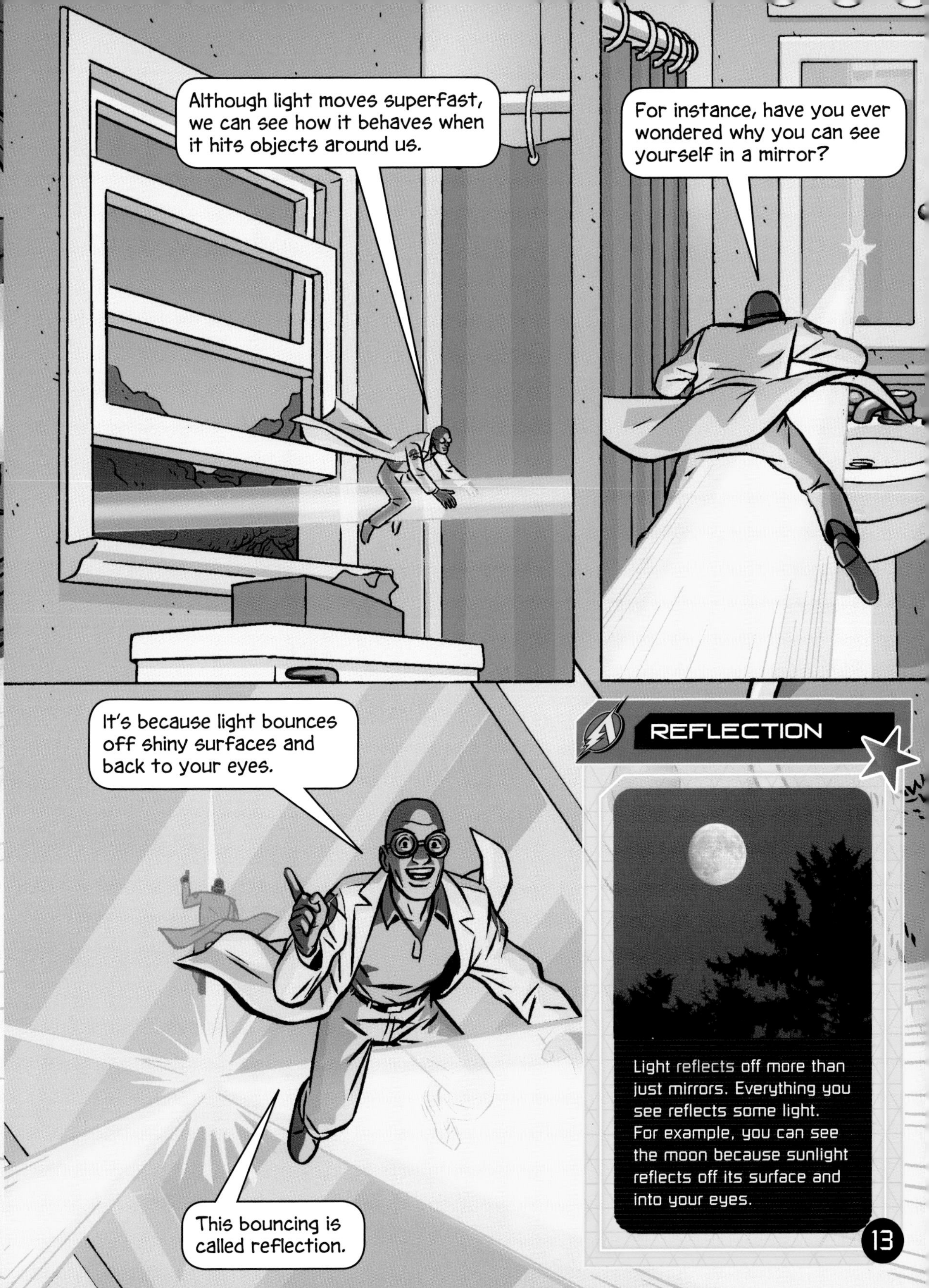
Although light moves superfast, we can see how it behaves when it hits objects around us.
For instance, have you ever wondered why you can see yourself in a mirror?
It's because light bounces off shiny surfaces and back to your eyes.
This bouncing is called reflection.

REFLECTION

Light reflects off more than just mirrors. Everything you see reflects some light. For example, you can see the moon because sunlight reflects off its surface and into your eyes.

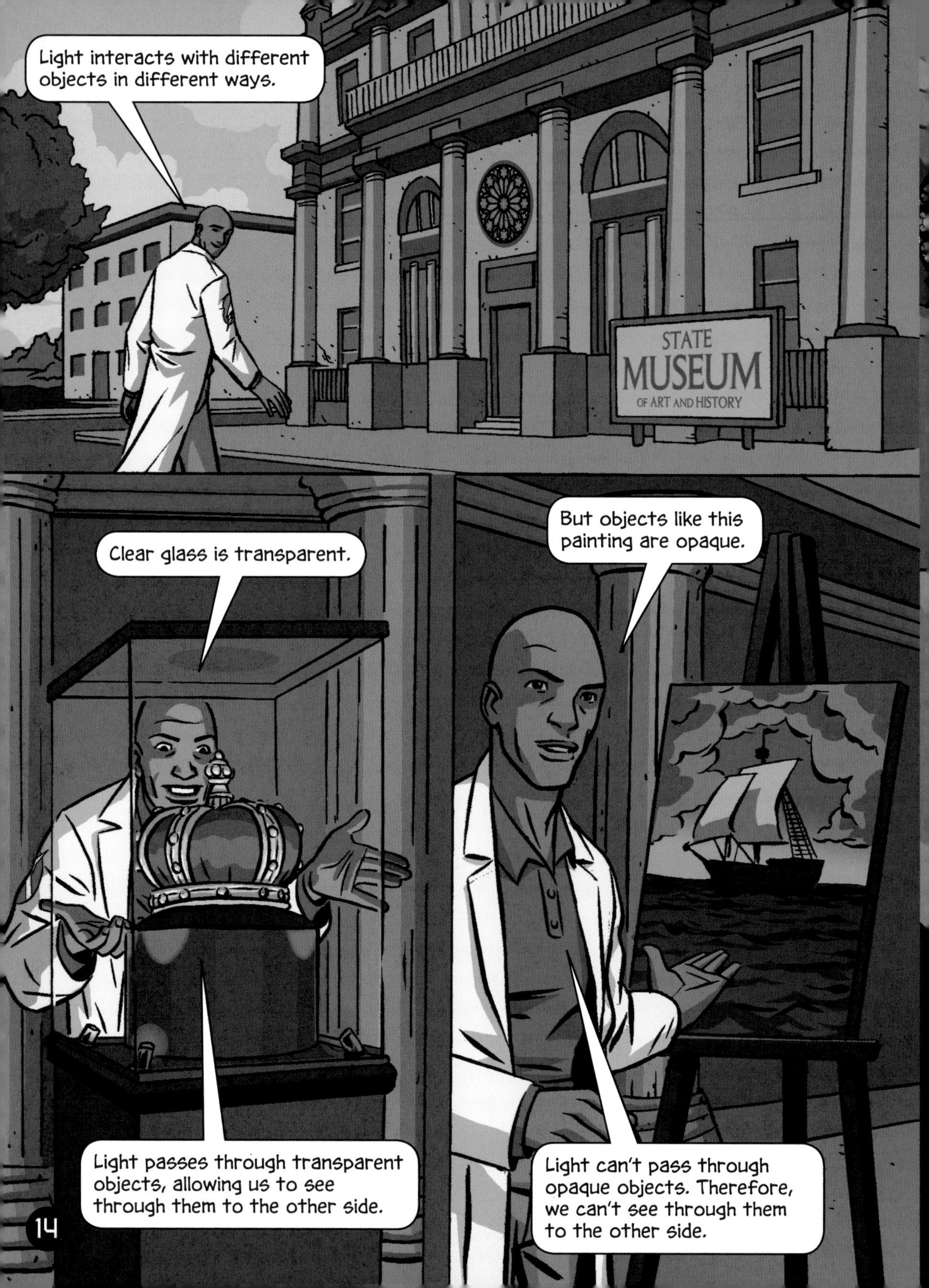
Light interacts with different objects in different ways.
STATE MUSEUM OF ART AND HISTORY
Clear glass is transparent.
Light passes through transparent objects, allowing us to see through them to the other side.
But objects like this painting are opaque.
Light can't pass through opaque objects. Therefore, we can't see through them to the other side.

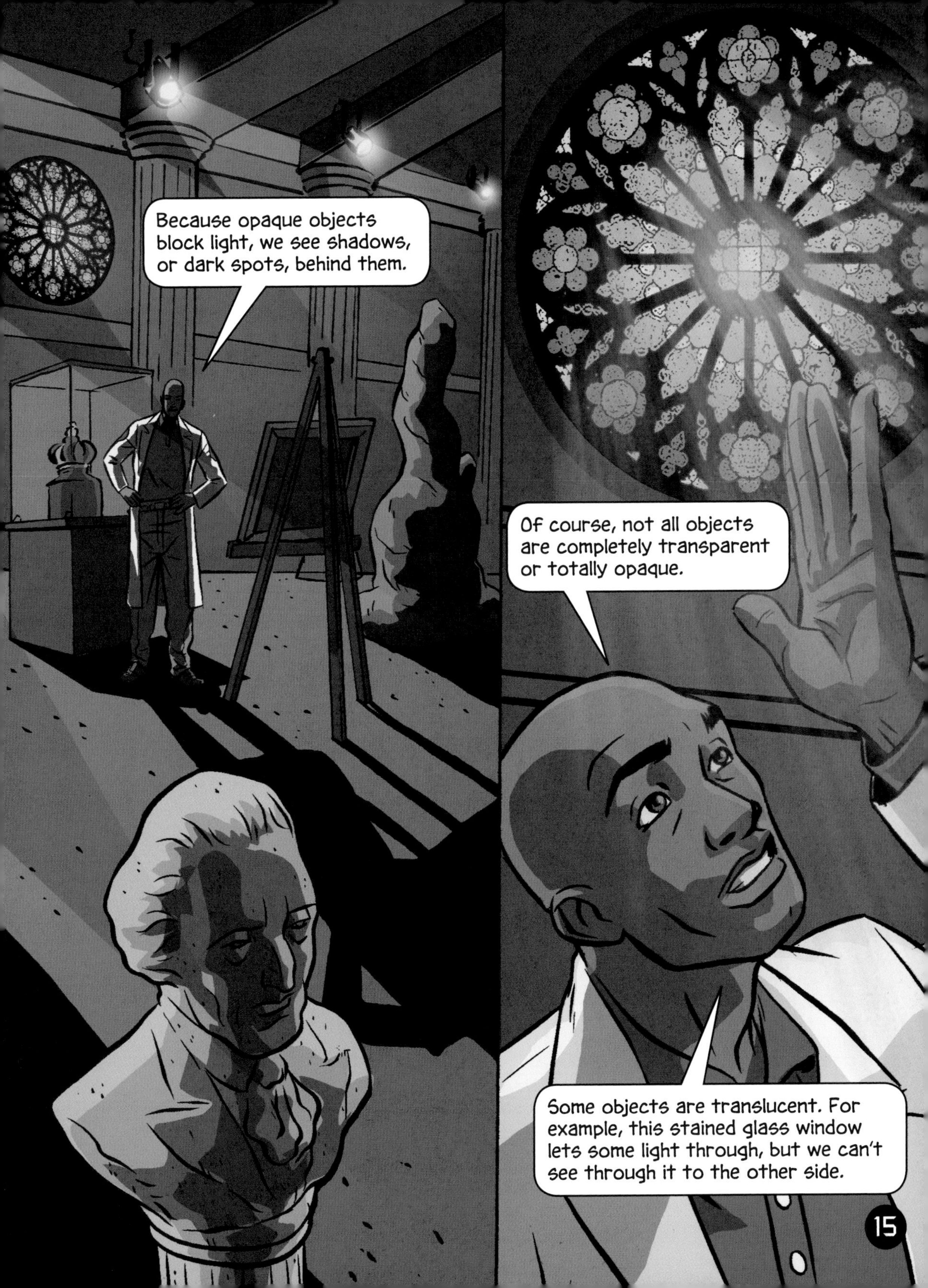
Because opaque objects block light, we see shadows, or dark spots, behind them.
Of course, not all objects are completely transparent or totally opaque.
Some objects are translucent. For example, this stained glass window lets some light through, but we can't see through it to the other side.

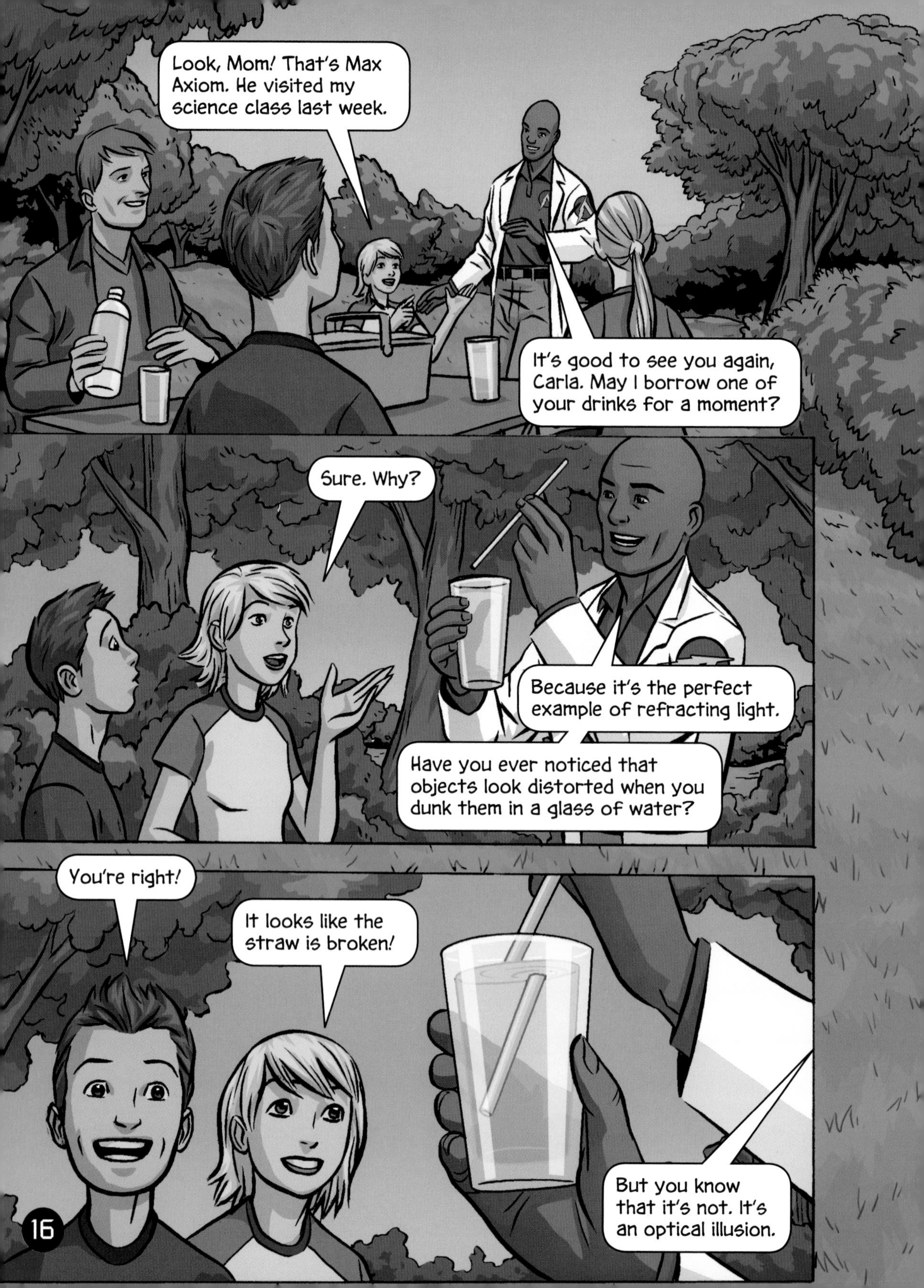
Look, Mom! That's Max Axiom. He visited my science class last week.
It's good to see you again, Carla. May I borrow one of your drinks for a moment?
Sure. Why?
Because it's the perfect example of refracting light.
Have you ever noticed that objects look distorted when you dunk them in a glass of water?
You're right!
It looks like the straw is broken!
But you know that it's not. It's an optical illusion.

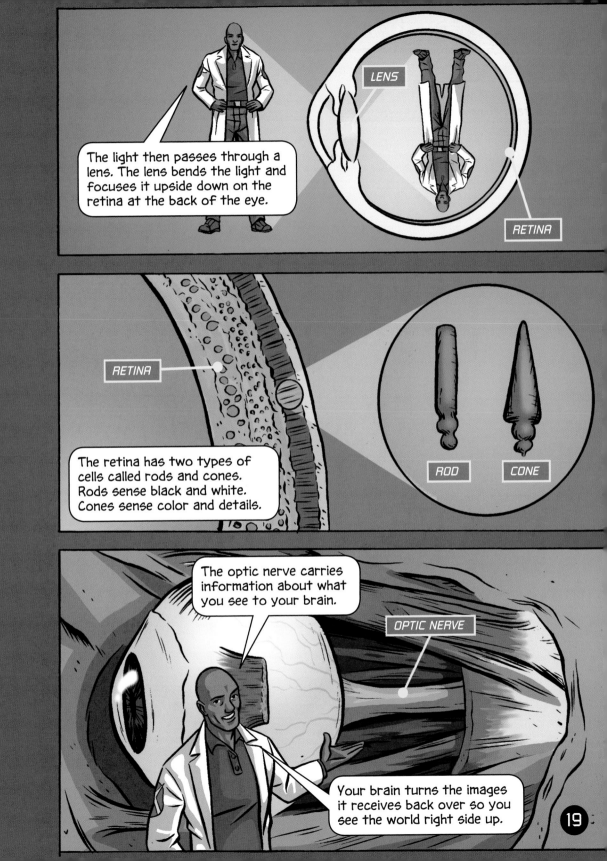

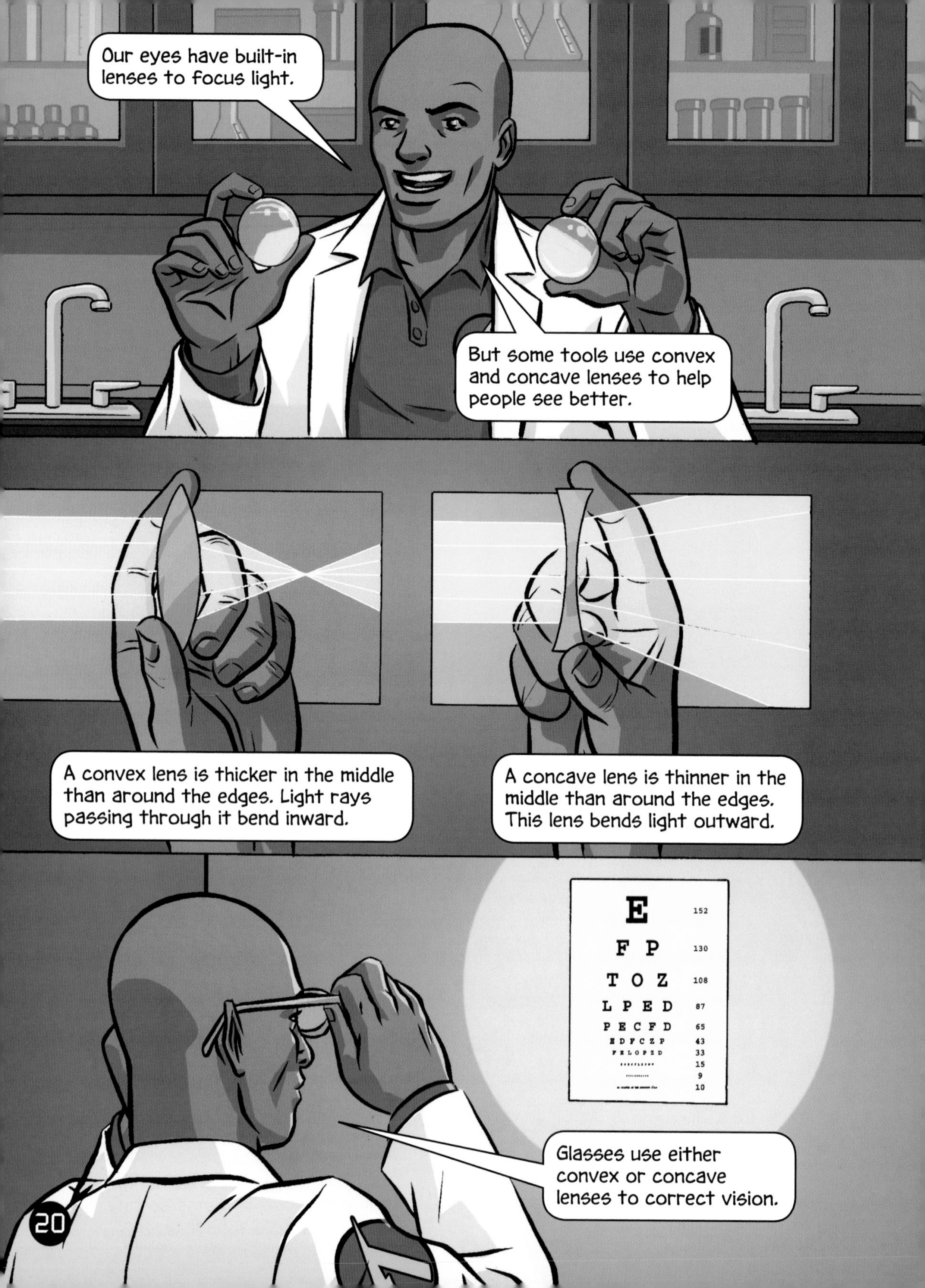
Our eyes have built-in lenses to focus light.
But some tools use convex and concave lenses to help people see better.
A convex lens is thicker in the middle than around the edges. Light rays passing through it bend inward.
A concave lens is thinner in the middle than around the edges. This lens bends light outward.
E 152
F P 130
T O Z 108
L P E D 87
P E C F D 65
E D F C Z P 43
F E L O P Z D 33
15
9
10
Glasses use either convex or concave lenses to correct vision.

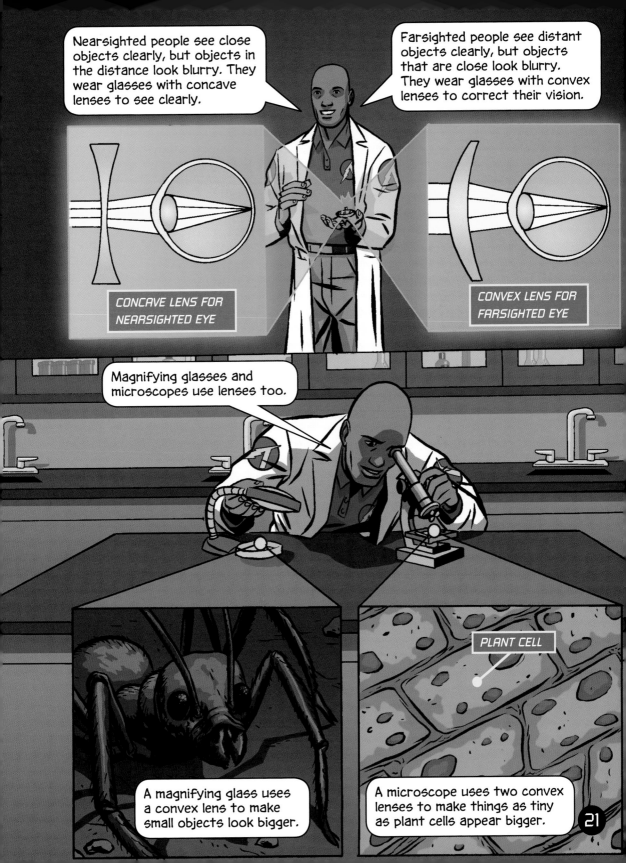

Nearsighted people see close objects clearly, but objects in the distance look blurry. They wear glasses with concave lenses to see clearly.

Farsighted people see distant objects clearly, but objects that are close look blurry. They wear glasses with convex lenses to correct their vision.

CONCAVE LENS FOR NEARSIGHTED EYE

CONVEX LENS FOR FARSIGHTED EYE

Magnifying glasses and microscopes use lenses too.

PLANT CELL

A magnifying glass uses a convex lens to make small objects look bigger.

A microscope uses two convex lenses to make things as tiny as plant cells appear bigger.

21

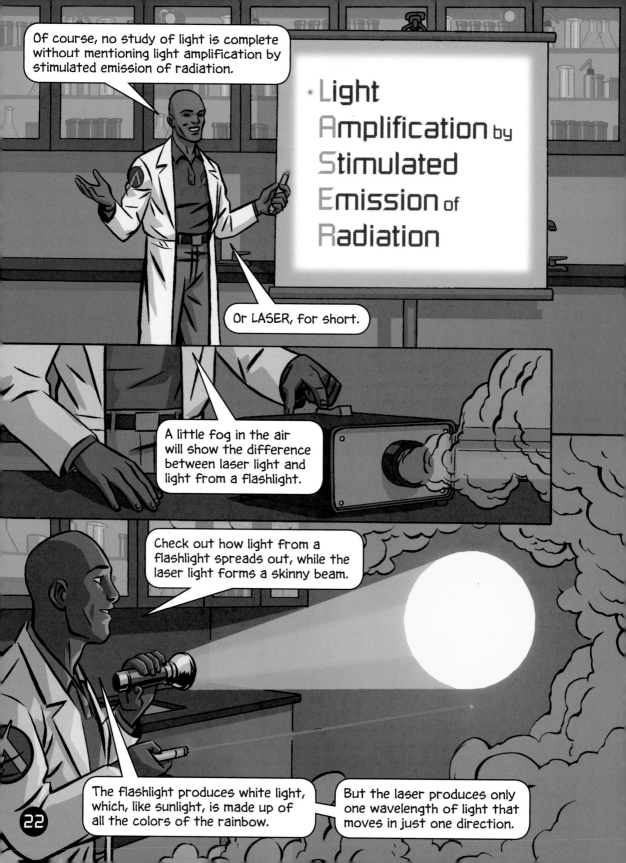

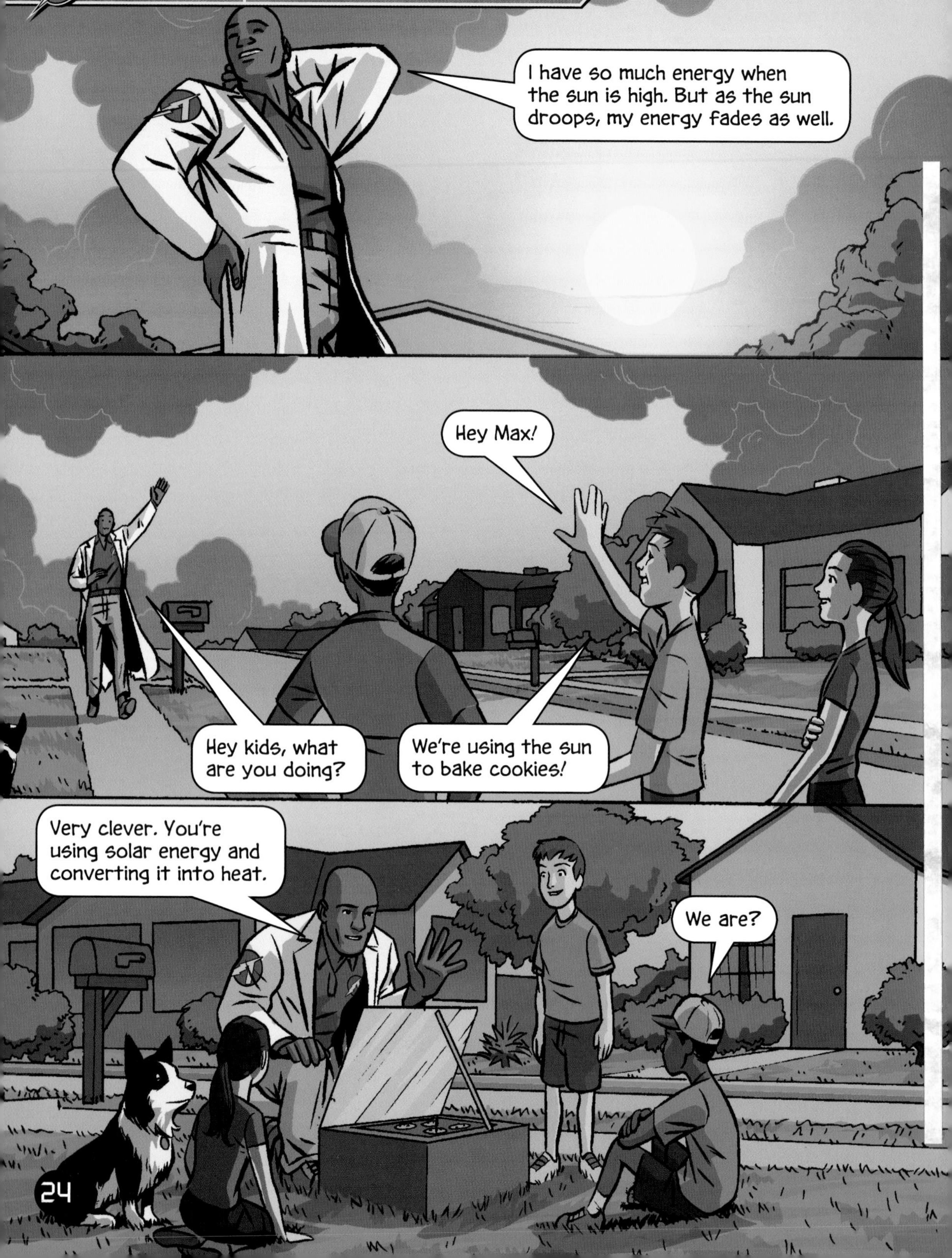
I have so much energy when the sun is high. But as the sun droops, my energy fades as well.
Hey Max!
Hey kids, what are you doing?
We're using the sun to bake cookies!
Very clever. You're using solar energy and converting it into heat.
We are?

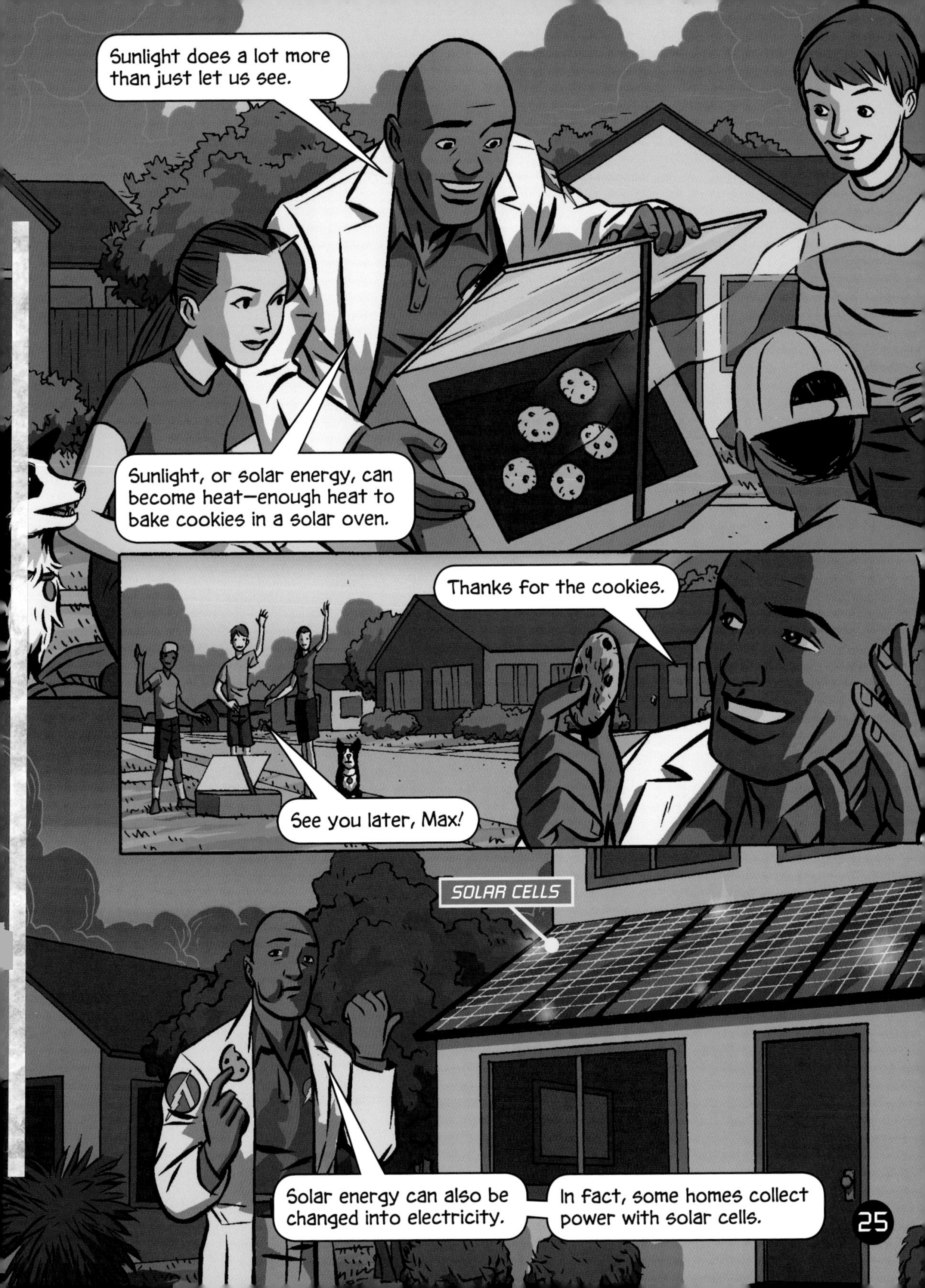
Sunlight does a lot more than just let us see.
Sunlight, or solar energy, can become heat—enough heat to bake cookies in a solar oven.
Thanks for the cookies.
See you later, Max!
SOLAR CELLS
Solar energy can also be changed into electricity.
In fact, some homes collect power with solar cells.

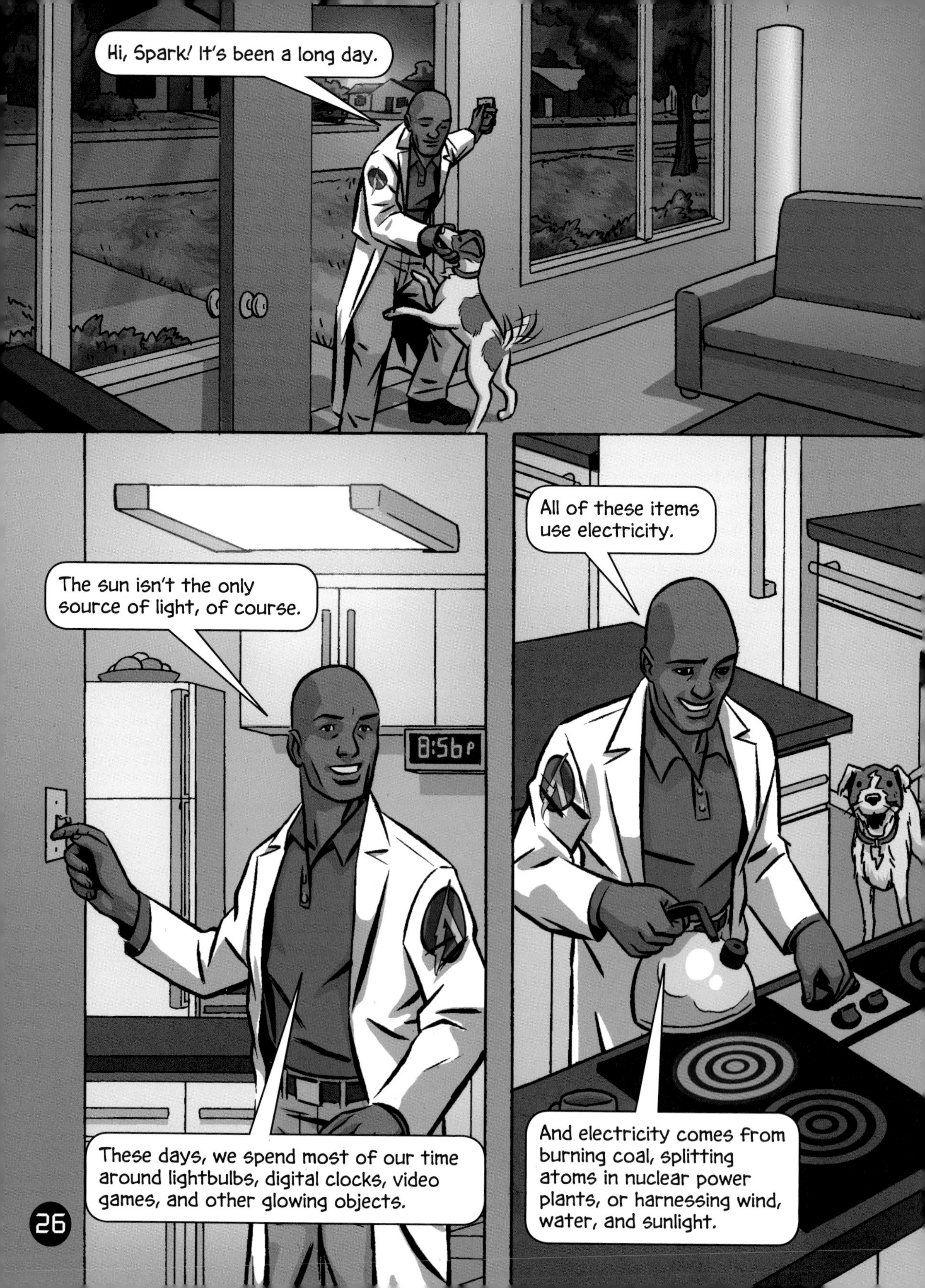
Hi, Spark! It's been a long day.
The sun isn't the only source of light, of course.
8:56 P
These days, we spend most of our time around lightbulbs, digital clocks, video games, and other glowing objects.
All of these items use electricity.
And electricity comes from burning coal, splitting atoms in nuclear power plants, or harnessing wind, water, and sunlight.

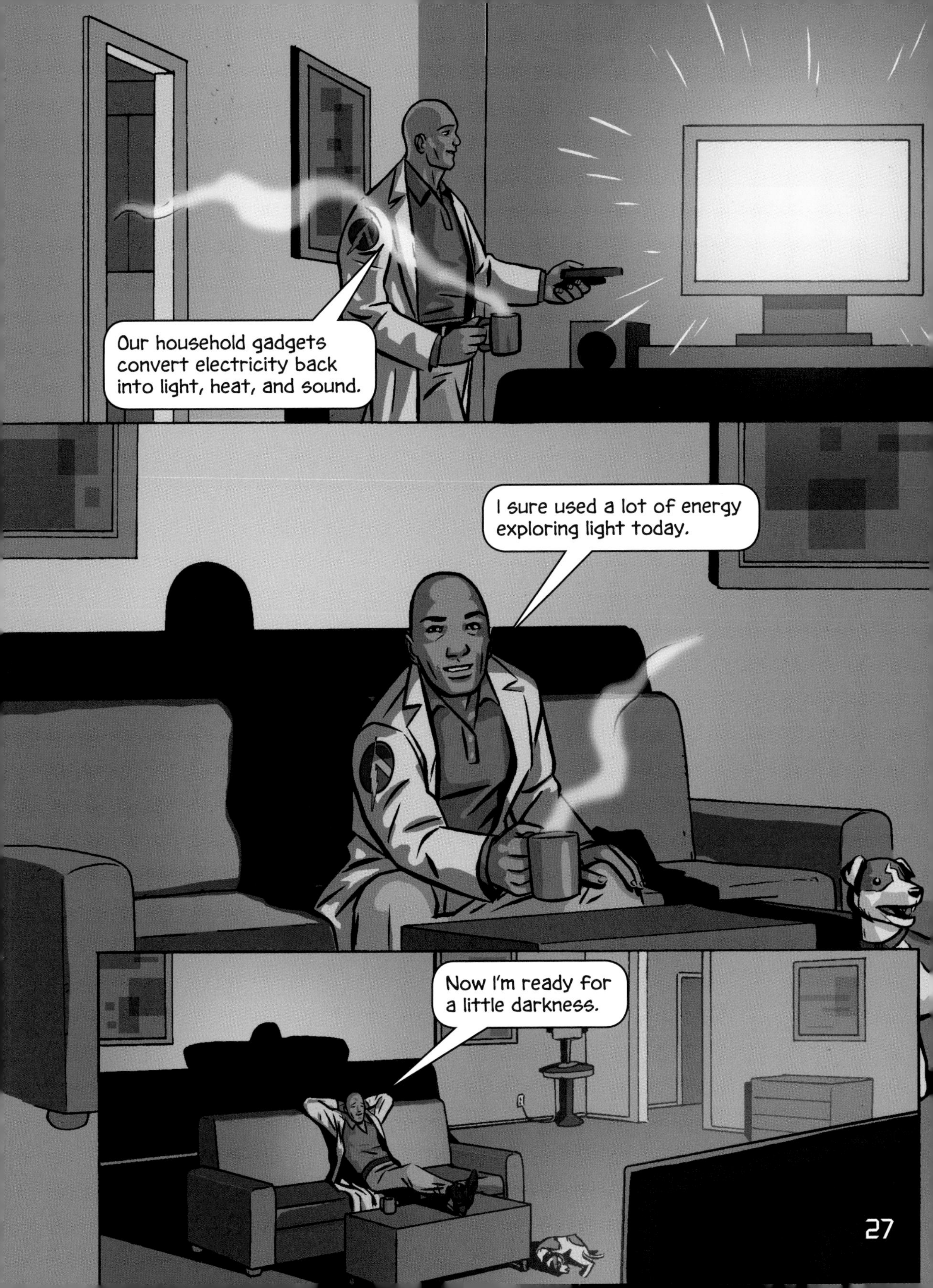
Our household gadgets convert electricity back into light, heat, and sound.
I sure used a lot of energy exploring light today.
Now I'm ready for a little darkness.

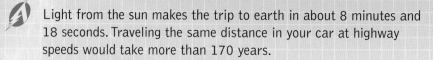

Light from the sun makes the trip to earth in about 8 minutes and 18 seconds. Traveling the same distance in your car at highway speeds would take more than 170 years.

Light changes speeds when it passes from one material to another. When light passes from air to water, it slows down to about 139,800 miles (225,000 km) per second.

The color of your T-shirt on a sunny, summer day can make a big difference in how hot you feel. Darker colors absorb more light than lighter colors. To stay cooler, wear a white T-shirt on a sunny day because it reflects more light than a darker shirt.

Only 10 percent of the energy used by a regular incandescent lightbulb is changed into visible light. The rest of the energy is wasted as heat.

Telescopes use lenses or mirrors to capture the little bits of light that come to earth from stars, planets, and galaxies in space. The Hubble Space Telescope has allowed us to see galaxies more than 12 billion light-years away.

Human eyes can sense light only within the visible wavelengths on the electromagnetic spectrum. Some animals see the world in a completely different way. Rattlesnakes have sensory pits that detect infrared light. Bees see ultraviolet light.

Moonbows are rainbows that form at night. These faint rainbows form when raindrops refract light reflecting off the moon. When moonlight refracts off ice crystals in the atmosphere, bright halos called moon dogs form around the moon.

Solar energy powers satellites and spacecraft orbiting earth. The *International Space Station*'s huge solar panels turn sunlight into electricity, light, and heat for the astronauts living and working on the spacecraft.

RAINBOW LIGHT

You don't need to wait for a rainstorm to spot a rainbow. Try this simple experiment to split white light into a rainbow of colors.

WHAT YOU NEED:

- black construction paper
- table
- clear drink glass
- water
- small mirror
- flashlight

WHAT YOU DO:

1. Place a piece of black construction paper on the table.
2. Place the glass in the center of the construction paper.
3. Fill the glass almost to the top with water.
4. Place the mirror at an angle inside the glass.
5. Turn off the lights and shine a flashlight through the glass so its light reflects off the mirror.
6. Adjust the position of the flashlight and the angle of the mirror until you see a rainbow appear on the construction paper.
7. Move the flashlight closer to and then farther from the glass of water to see how small and large you can make your rainbow.

DISCUSSION QUESTIONS

1. Based on the illustration at the top of page 9, which types of energy in the electromagnetic spectrum have the longest waves? Which have the shortest? How can you tell?

2. What happens to white light when it passes through a prism? Describe a time when you saw the same thing happen in nature.

3. What role does reflection play in our ability to see objects? Give an example to support your answer.

4. What are the differences between transparent, opaque, and translucent objects? Look around the room and see if you can find examples of each one.

WRITING PROMPTS

1. Based on what you've learned, draw a diagram that helps explain how light passing through raindrops creates a rainbow. Add labels to your diagram to help explain what is happening.

2. The sun is the earth's biggest source of energy. But what would happen if the sun suddenly vanished? Write a paragraph describing what life would be like on earth without light.

3. Lenses bend, or refract, light in different ways. Make a list of all the things you know that use lenses. See if you can come up with at least 10!

4. Imagine that you could travel at the speed of light! What would you do with this superpower? Write a short story detailing your adventures using this amazing power!

TAKE A QUIZ!

atom (AT-uhm)—an element in its smallest form

concave (kahn-KAYV)—hollow and curved, like the inside of a bowl

convex (kahn-VEKS)—curved outward, like the outside of a ball

energy (EN-ur-jee)—the ability to do work, such as moving things or giving heat or light

fusion (FYOO-zhuhn)—the joining together of objects caused by heating; the sun creates its energy with the process of fusion

infrared light (IN-fruh-red LITE)—light that produces heat; humans cannot see infrared light

laser (LAY-zur)—a thin, intense, high-energy beam of light

opaque (oh-PAKE)—blocking light

reflection (ree-FLEK-shuhn)—the change in direction of light bouncing off a surface

refract (ree-FRACT)—to bend light as it passes through a substance at an angle

translucent (trans-LOO-suhnt)—letting light pass through, but not transparent; frosted and stained glass are translucent

transparent (transs-PAIR-uhnt)—letting light through

ultraviolet light (uhl-truh-VYE-uh-lit LITE)—an invisible form of light that can cause sunburns

wavelength (WAYV-length)—the distances between two peaks of a wave

READ MORE

Braun, Eric. *Curious Pearl Investigates Light.* Curious Pearl, Science Girl. North Mankato, Minn.: Picture Window Books, 2018.

Connors, Kathleen. *Light and Color.* A Look at Physical Science. New York: Gareth Stevens Publishing, 2018.

Crane, Cody. *Light.* Rookie Read-About Science. New York: Children's Press, 2019.

Spilsbury, Richard. *Investigating Light.* Investigating Science Challenges. New York: Crabtree Publishing, 2018.

Use Facthound to find Internet sites related to this book.

Visit *www.facthound.com*

Just type in 9781543558685 and go!

Check out projects, games and lots more at
www.capstonekids.com

INDEX